£27

Settle To Carlisle

The threatened

CW01604199

Colin Ha

The aim of this book is to portray the Settle to Carlisle line through a difficult period in its life. Closure was being actively promoted by British Rail with all freight and long distance passenger services diverted to other routes. All the stations on the line except Settle and Appleby had been closed. The train service had been reduced to two each way. Against this was an impressive array of local authorities and other bodies fighting the proposal. Putting their money where their mouths were a local service was reinstated. Using specially chartered trains the aim was to encourage tourism with walkers and people just wanting to travel the line to see its scenic splendour. Backed by an overwhelmingly successful promotion campaign the line started to thrive. Some special excursions started to be steam hauled as British Rail withdrew their "steam ban" from this line. As thousands of people flocked to the line the decline went into reverse. At first passenger trains had to be lengthened to cope. Then an extra train had to be run in each direction. Finally the excessive cost quoted by British Rail for maintaining the Ribblehead Viaduct was debunked to a more realistic and affordable figure. The line was eventually reprieved.

This book is dedicated to all those who fought to keep it open.

Colin Hall 2003.

PHOTOGRAPHS

FRONT COVER	The "Volcano" erupts. Living up to its nickname former Southern Railway "West Country" class pacific 34092 "City of Wells" storms through Ribblehead station with a northbound Cumbrian Mountain Pullman.	30/4/83
FRONTISPIECE	Southern Railway 4-6-0 No 850 "Lord Nelson" climbs from Selside on a northbound Cumbrian Mountain Express.	25/2/84
BACK COVER	Class 25 B0-B0 diesel electric No 25198 backs into Appleby Station over the connection with the former North Eastern Railway Line from Tebay to Darlington. By the time of this photograph it had been reduced to a short branch to serve an MOD depot at Warcop from which this train had just returned.	27/2/84

Colin Hall Publishing
Fordingbridge
Hampshire

1&2 Two views of the main station building at Settle of typical Midland Railway design. This was the first station of the "long drag" climb of 1 in 50 from Settle Junction a mile to the south where the line leaves that of the Leeds to Lancaster, to the summit at Blea Moor. The set of wooden steps are to help passengers into the trains from the low platform.

Date not recorded.

3&4 Two further views of the fine collection of Midland Railway buildings at Settle. The signal box had been closed by the time of the photograph with this section now controlled by the box at Settle Junction. The goods yard closed in 1970. The grand water tower shows the importance of Settle as a watering point for steam locomotives in the stations heyday.

Date not recorded.

5 Class 40 1Co-Co1 diesel electric locomotive 40135 waits to depart Settle with the 15:55 Leeds to Carlisle. The driver looks back to see the guards green flag as the tip to start.

1/8/84

6 Class 47 Co-Co diesel electric locomotive 47136 arrives at Settle with the 09:00 Leeds to Carlisle. The redundant signal box and post devoid of signal arms shows the run down state of the line.

2/8/84

7&8 Two views of the return working of the previous train seen in 6. 47136 arrives and departs Settle with the 16:35 Carlisle to Leeds train. Of note is the old Midland wooden signal post devoid of starter arm to the left of the arriving train.

2/8/84

9&10 A pair of 2 car dmus arrives and departs Settle as a summer relief service from York to Carlisle. A good sprinkling of passengers line the platform despite the rain. The lead unit is a class 110 "Calder Valley" unit whilst a Metro-Cammell class 101 takes up the rear.

2/8/84

11 As dusk falls class 25 Bo-Bo diesel electric locomotive 25060 enters Settle with the 16:00 Leeds to Carlisle. This was unusual motive power and would have been a last minute replacement for a loco which had failed on the outward run.

29/10/83

12 Just north of Settle the line passes the village of Langcliffe. There was never a station here but a private siding served a small quarry. 25060 passes running very late with the 10:40 Carlisle to Leeds, the outward working of that seen in the previous photo.

29/10/83

13 Class 31s were seen for a while on workings from York. The unusual working seen here with 31190 is a sandite train. A special wagon carrying a tank with a solution containing sand which is sprayed onto the track to improve adhesion. It is especially important during the period when autumn leaves on the track are a problem. It is seen passing Langcliffe northbound.

29/10/83

14 Also northbound at the same location 47424 storms north on a special excursion. The hut on the left marks the site of the private siding into the quarry.

29/10/83

15 Further north the line passes Helwith Bridge with the River Ribble running alongside. A flock of birds scatter from the field as 47104 roars pass as it gets to grip with the 1 in 50 climb hauling the morning Leeds to Carlisle train.

25/2/84

16 Also at Helwith Bridge we see former Southern Railway 4-6-0 No 850 “Lord Nelson” on a northbound Cumbrian Mountain Express. This locomotive was built at Eastleigh in 1926.

3/8/85

17 Heading north Horton in Ribblesdale is the next station. A pair of class 31s in double harness, 31183 and 31184 climb through the station with a Leeds to Carlisle football special. The siding leading off to the right serves a quarry.

3/12/83

18 47436 races downhill, through Horton in Ribblesdale station, with the 10:40 Carlisle to Leeds. The station sidings are controlled from this excellent example of a Midland Railway signal box seen on the right.

3/12/83

19 Above Horton in Ribblesdale, on a very misty day, a two car Metro Cammell class 101 dmu rattles north. It was probably a "Q" train. These were special workings run ahead of steam excursions by the British Transport Police. This was to combat the excessive and often reckless trespass on the line by some enthusiasts.

23/2/85

20&21 Two views of the steam special running behind the "Q" train in 19. With really awful Weather closing in two ex LMS 4-6-0s, "black 5" No 44767 and "Jubilee" No 5690 climb north. Horton in Ribblesdale station can be seen in the background. The number of car borne visitors flocking to see these trains causes chaos on the narrow roads as can be seen in the foreground.

23/2/85

22 Southern Railway No 850 "Lord Nelson" is again seen, this time climbing north above the village of Selside with a Cumbrian Mountain Express.

25/2/84

23 Another view of No 850 "Lord Nelson" climbing above Selside towards Ribblehead.
25/2/84

24 Former LMS Stanier Pacific 46229 "Duchess of Hamilton" blasts out of the mist and rain as she approaches Ribblehead station. She is nearing the end of the climb from Settle and is hauling the Cumbrian Mountain Pullman northbound. "Duchess of Hamilton" was built at Crewe in 1938.

4/2/84

25 Former Southern Railway Bullied Pacific 34092 "City of Wells" in full cry near the top of the climb to Ribblehead with a northbound Cumbrian Mountain Pullman. "City of Wells" was built at Brighton in 1949 so entered service just after nationalisation so was always a "BR" loco. Whist most of this class were rebuilt in the 1950s she still remains in original condition with "airsmooth" semi-streamlining.

3/12/85

26&27 A pair of class 20 Bo-Bo diesel electric locomotives pass through Ribblehead station northbound on a special railtour. They sport the then new “Railfreight” livery of grey body, yellow wrap round ends and red frames. The line in the forground leads into Ribblehead Quarry.

3/8/85

28&29 Two views of a "Dalesrail" special passing through Ribblehead station. Northbound trains could not call at Ribblehead at this time because the platform on this side had been removed to provide better rail access to the quarry. The train is formed mostly of class 101 2-car Metro-Cammell dmus but a solitary Birmingham RCW class 104 unit brings up the rear. This is still in the older all over blue livery of the late 1960s.

3/8/84

30 On a really miserable morning two class 40 locomotives, 40079 and 40181, approach Ribblehead on a special excursion.

Date not recorded

31 47571 accelerates away from the speed restriction after crossing Ribblehead Viaduct and passes through Ribblehead station with the 10:45 Carlisle to Leeds.

3/8/85

32 The sheep ignore 47104 as it crosses the embankment linking Ribblehead station to the viaduct with an excursion from Yeovil to Carlisle.

21/4/84

33 47487 comes off Ribblehead Viaduct and starts to accelerate southwards with a special excursion returning to North Walsham in Norfolk.

21/4/84

34 SR 4-6-0 850 "Lord Nelson" cautiously approaches Ribblehead Viaduct with a northbound Cumbrian Mountain Pullman.

3/8/85

35 SR "West Country" 34092 "City of Wells" takes a northbound Cumbrian Mountain Pullman round the curved embankment between station and viaduct at Ribblehead.

30/4/83

36 A close up of the tall slender arches of Ribblehead Viaduct. The white squares are the notices warning of falling masonry. The viaduct is also known as Battymoss Viaduct after the area it crosses.

Date not recorded

37 47104 creeps across the viaduct with a Yeovil to Carlisle excursion.

21/4/84

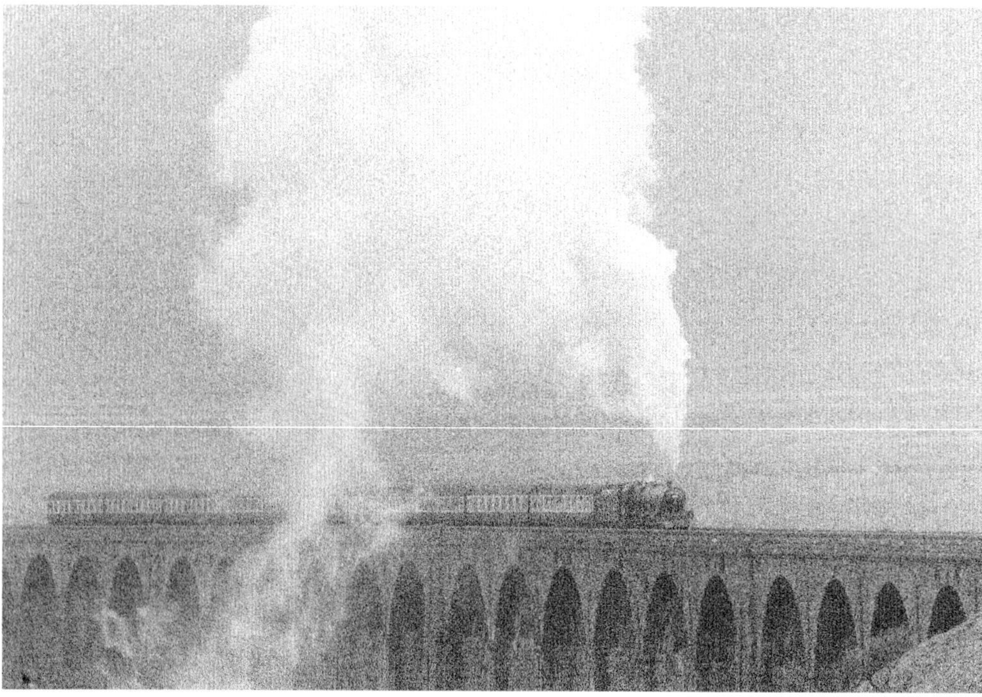

38 The strong wind and rain snatches the exhaust from ex-LMS "Jubilee" 5690 "Leander" as it crosses the viaduct with a northbound special.

16/10/82

39 Continuing from the previous shot "Leander" is now clear of the viaduct and accelerates pass the loops at Blea Moor summit.

16/10/82

40 A class 47 passes the loops at Blea Moor with the 10:00 Carlisle to Leeds.

16/10/82

41 Deputising for a failed "Leander" ex-LMS "Black 5" 4-6-0 5407 rounds the curve from Ribblehead Viaduct to the summit at Blea Moor with a northbound Cumbrian Mountain Pullman.

17/8/83

42 LMS Pacific 46229 "Duchess of Hamilton" storms pass the loops at Blea Moor with a northbound Cumbrian Mountain Express.

29/10/83

43 A stranger on the Settle & Carlisle. An HST set is signalled for the up loop at Blea Moor on a private charter. Blea Moor Tunnel can be seen in the distance.

44 The HST set runs into the loop at Blea Moor. This shot clearly shows the up and down loops with their attendant signal box. It also vividly shows the total isolation of this location surrounded by brooding, barren hills.

45 Passengers on the HST get a grandstand view as LMS Stanier Pacific 46229 "Duchess of Hamilton" storms through Blea Moor northbound.

46 Taking up the rear is a former LNWR Directors or Royal saloon. The Pullman ahead of it is a Metro-Cammell vehicle built for the East Coast mainline in the early 60s. Unfortunately I do not have a date for this sequence of photographs.

47 An unusual feature at Blea Moor is this aqueduct taking the River Ribble over the railway line.

48&49 The northern end of Blea Moor tunnel opens out into Denthead. The line undulates from here to Ais Gill which is the summit of the southbound climb. In these views BR standard 9F 2-10-0 92220 "Evening Star" crosses Denthead Viaduct with a northbound special. The steam locomotive is famous for being the last built for BR emerging from Swindon Works in 1960.

21/4/84

50&51 A dull day sees a doubleheaded southbound Cumbrian Mountain Pullman approaching and crossing Denthead Viaduct. The locomotives are ex-SR "King Arthur" class 4-6-0 777 "Sir Lamiel" and ex-LMS "Black 5" 4-6-0 5407. The fences on the hillside in the background are to hold back the snow in winter.

Date not recorded.

52 Dent station is the highest in England and is several miles from the village of that name. On a very murky day ex-LNER Gresley A4 pacific 4498 "Sir Nigel Gresley" storms through the station with a northbound Cumbrian Mountain Express. This locomotive was built at Doncaster in 1937 and carries the name of the designer of this famous class.

13/10/84

53 47456 speeds through the station with the 10:40 Carlisle to Leeds. The white patch d on the bridge indicates a signal once stood here. The white square would have been painted so that the signal arm stood out clearly making it more visible to the drivers of approaching trains.

13/20/84

54&55 In these two views SR Bullied pacific 34092 "City of Wells" sweeps round the curve into Dent station with a southbound Cumbrian Mountain Pullman. Taken a year before the previous two shots you can clearly see the old Midland Railway signal box beyond the station which had since been demolished.

20/11/83

56&57 These two show BR standard 9F 2-10-0 92220 "Evening Star" departing from Garsdale station and heading north with a Cumbrian Mountain Express. Garsdale was an important watering stop for these specials. In former times it had been the junction of a branch to Hawes and because of this it had been named Hawes Junction for many years. Its real claim to fame is the story of an engine being turned on the turntable which used to be here. It was caught by the wind and spun out of control. The viaduct seen here was built as a replacement for an embankment which collapsed soon after the line first opened.

21/4/84

58 Class 45 1Co-Co1 diesel electric 45122 passes beneath the footbridge at the crossing at Lunds. There was no station here, the crossing taking its name from the nearby hamlet. The train is the 09:07 Leeds to Carlisle. This train was booked to run with four carriages but had been strengthened on this occasion to convey Leeds United supporters for a game against Carlisle. The growing popularity of the S&C from this time following the publicity surrounding the proposed closure meant that trains had to be progressively lengthened.

3/12/83

59 SR pacific 34092 "City of Wells" appears out of the gloom near Lunds on a northbound Cumbrian Mountain Pullman.

3/12/83

60&61 A southbound double headed steam special breasts the summit at Ais Gill. The train is hauled by ex-LNER K1 2-6-0 2005 built by the North British Co, Glasgow in 1949 and ex-LMS "Black 5" 4-6-0 4767 a Crewe product of 1947. The signal box had not long closed hence the posts devoid of arms and loops still in situ. The antics of the "enthusiasts" on the bridge show why the police had to take to special trains as noted in photo 19.

Date not recorded

62 45142 passes the summit at Ais Gill with the 16:35 Carlisle to Leeds. Compare with the two previous photographs. The signal box, posts and loops have all been swept away. The stepped mountain in the background is "Wild Boar Fell" so named as it is reputed to be where the last wild boar in England was killed.

21/4/84

63 45150 passes the site of Ais Gill signal box with the 16:00 Leeds to Carlisle. The empty formation in the foreground shows where the down loop was situated. The corrugated iron hut peering out of the tall grass on the right once housed the signal lamps and oil.

21/4/84

64 Looking very forlorn prior to removal is the old Midland Railway box at Ais Gill for so long a major landmark on the line. The summit here marked the highest point on the line and the end of the long climb at 1 in 50 south from Appleby. Loops were provided here so express passenger trains could overtake slow freights.

65 A double headed southbound Cumbrian Mountain Pullman approaches Ais Gill hauled by ex SR "King Arthur" class 4-6-0 777 "Sir Lamiel" and ex LMS "Black 5" 4-6-0 5407.

Date not recorded

66 Bullied pacific 34092 "City of Wells" storms up the last few yards towards the summit at Ais Gill with a southbound Cumbrian Mountain Pullman. Not all is well with the locomotive as the smokebox door is glowing red hot and the paint has flaked off.

20/11/82

67&68 Ex LNER Gresley A4 pacific 60009 "Union of South Africa" approaches Birkett Tunnel with a southbound Cumbrian Mountain Express. This locomotive was built at Doncaster in 1937.

31/3/84

69 The old Midland Railway station at Kirkby Stephen West was closed at the time of these photographs and had been since 1970. The "West" part if its name was to differentiate from the North Eastern Railway station on the other side of town which was known as Kirkby Stephen East.

9/6/84

70 46229 "Duchess of Hamilton" has steam to spare with its safety valves blowing as it climbs through Kirkby Stephen with a southbound Cumbrian Mountain Express. The old goods yard was being used by a local road haulier and the goods shed was still standing. The some sidings were still in use by the Permanent Way Dept but freight ceased here in 1964.

9/6/84

71 A pair of class 31 A1A-A1A diesel electrics, 31445 and 31466, pass through Kirkby Stephen station with the 16:35 Carlisle to Hull. Despite being closed for 15 years the station buildings looked in very good order.

2/8/85

72 40122 became a celebrity locomotive when it was repainted in BR green with original number D200. It was later retained for preservation as part of the national collection. It is seen coasting downhill through Kirkby Stephen with the afternoon Leeds to Carlisle service. Note the signal box is not an original Midland one but of modern design.

2/8/85

73&74 46229 "Duchess of Hamilton" is seen catching the last light of day as she heads south near Ormside. She sports a "Royal Scot" headboard recalling the glory days of these locomotives on the crack London Euston to Glasgow expresses.

8/12/84

75 A class 45 locomotive climbs away from Ormside Viaduct with a special utilising the restored Pullmans of the Venice Simplon Orient Express.

8/12/84

76 In contrast on a bright sunny day 47104 climbs near Ormside with an excursion returning from Carlisle to Yeovil.

21/4/84

77 On the southern outskirts of Appleby a northbound morning service approaches hauled by 47592.

8/12/84

78 On a better day a pair of Derby Twin dmus climb from Appleby towards Helm Tunnel with a special Christmas shoppers charter to Skipton, Keighley and Leeds.

3/12/83

79 Appleby has always been the most important station on the line and this is reflected in the buildings. The main building housing the booking office is on the down side. Note the elaborate bargeboards and iron tracery in the windows.

27/2/84

80 On the up side stands a large waiting room again with elaborate bargeboards. Original Midland Railway platform seats are still in use with their "rustic" ironwork.

27/2/84

81 No prizes for guessing which end of the station Appleby North box stands. The "South" box had gone by this time. This box is not entirely original Midland having been rebuilt by the LMS. Note the old lamp half way along the front. This box controls the station and the link to the old North Eastern line which was open to Warcop at this time.

27/2/84

82 A curious building in Appleby yard. Was this an old signal box now in use as an office?

27/2/84

83&84 Two further examples of old Midland Railway buildings still in use at Appleby.
27/2/84

85 45142 runs into the station with the 09:07 Leeds to Carlisle. Note the old goods shed in the background. The goods yard closed in 1971.

27/2/84

86 A Derby Twin dmu arrives at Appleby under the graceful wrought iron footbridge and a heavy fall of snow. This train was running only as far as Skipton because of engineering works between there and Leeds.

23/3/80

87 As the dmu departs a class 40 emerges from the blizzard with train of sand.

23/3/80

88 The class 40 trundles on through towards Carlisle.

23/3/80

89 Later that day a 3 car Metro-Cammell dmu draws out of Appleby on a Skipton to Carlisle working. The unit is in the short lived livery of all over white with blue waist band. The water containers on the platform are waiting to be despatched to Blea Moor signal box. This was the boxes only supply of water.

23/3/80

90 25198 stands in Appleby station waiting a pathway north to Carlisle after a trip working to Warcop on the old North Eastern line.

27/2/84

91 31435 runs in with the summer additional Carlisle to York service. Note the Mk2 coaching stock which was a rarity on the line. All regular services being composed of Mk1 BR coaching stock.

3/8/85

92 45132 speeds through with an excursion returning to Leicester. Note the complete rake of Mk2 Inter-City coaches complete with an air conditioned brake immediately behind the locomotive. This was in effect a complete St Pancras - Nottingham / Sheffield train of the time transplanted onto the S&C.

21/4/84

93 A 2 car Derby dmu at Appleby on a "Dalesrail" special working to Leeds.

3/8/85

94 45005 enters Appleby station with the 10:40 Carlisle to Leeds.

27/2/84

95 45017 passes through with a special from Exeter.

16/10/82

96 North of Appleby the landscape broadens out. A class 47 approaches with the morning Carlisle to Leeds service.

20/11/82

97 D200/40122 - The Green 40 - accelerates away from its Appleby stop with a northbound Cumbrian Mountain Express. D200 was deputising for a steam locomotive. Steam bans were imposed, often at very short notice, during prolonged hot dry spells because of the risk of line side fires.

9/6/84

98 Winter sunshine catches a class 31 as it leaves Appleby heading north with the morning Leeds to Carlisle train.

20/11/82

99 LNER A4 pacific 4498 "Sir Nigel Gresley" is seen in full cry heading north near Long Marston with a Cumbrian Mountain Pullman.

13/10/84

100&101 New Biggin station showing the main station building and waiting shelter. It had closed in 1970 so some fifteen years later when these pictures were taken they looked in good order. The station clock was still in place.

31/3/84

102 A class 45 speeds through the closed station of New Biggin with the 0907 Leeds to Carlisle.

31/3/84

103 SR "West Country" pacific 34092 "City of Wells" crosses New Biggin Viaduct with a southbound Cumbrian Mountain Pullman.

20/11/82

104 A4 pacific 60009 "Union of South Africa" approaches the former station at New Biggin on a southbound Cumbrian Mountain Express.

31/3/84

105 LMS Stanier pacific 46229 "Duchess of Hamilton" passes through the closed at Culgaith with a southbound Cumbrian Mountain Express. The old station building can be seen behind the locomotive and the signal box was still in use controlling the level crossing.

9/6/84

106 BR standard 9F 2-10-0 92220 "Evening Star" speeds through Culgaith bound for Carlisle.

21/4/84

107 47487 passes through Culgaith with a North Walsham to Carlisle excursion. This view was taken looking down from over the tunnel mouth and shows the old station, signal box and level crossing in the background.

29/12/83

108 A class 47 emerges from Barons Wood Tunnel with a Nottingham to Glasgow train.
Date not recorded

109 Ex LMS “Black 5” 5305 rounds the curve near Howe & Co Siding on the climb south from Carlisle with a “Santa Special”.

29/12/83

110 The 09:07 Leeds to Carlisle service hauled by 45122 near Howe and Co Siding south of Carlisle.

29/12/83

111&112 Two views of the former station at Cumwhinton, the first station out from Carlisle on the S&C. It closed to all traffic in 1956 but like most of the former stations on the line has withstood the ravishes of time well.

29/12/83

113 The station masters house ,and behind it the cottages of the lower ranks stand on higher ground overlooking the station to which the steps in the left foreground lead down.

29/12/83

114 47562 heads the 10:40 Carlisle to Leeds through Cumwhinton.

29/12/83

115 Carlisle - journeys end. 40035 in Carlisle Citadel station awaiting its next turn of duty. Originally named “Apapa” with a cast nameplate when new, this had been reinstated in paint on the bodysides. The class 40s served the S&C well throughout their careers on both passenger and freight ousting steam and now in their own final days.

9/6/84

116 A class 26 Bo-Bo locomotive 26028 stands at the head of a train to Glasgow via Dumfries. A reminder that Carlisle is not far from the Scottish border and that in the heyday of the S&C many expresses ran through to Glasgow by this route.

Date not known